**DO NOT REMOVE
CARDS FROM POCKET**

LET'S TALK ABOUT
BEING BOSSY

By Joy Berry
Illustrated by John Costanza

CHILDRENS PRESS®
CHICAGO

Let's talk about BEING BOSSY.

Bossy people want to have
their way all the time.

Bossy people think they know
what is best for everyone.
They think they know what
everyone should and should not do.

Bossy people tell others
what to do and expect them
to do what they are told to do.

Bossy people expect others to obey them.

Some bossy people try to
bribe others into obeying.

They promise to give something
to the people who obey them.

Some bossy people try to
threaten others into obeying.

They say that they will go away or not
play with the people who will not obey them.

13

Some bossy people try to
frighten others into obeying.

They act as though they will hurt
the people who will not obey them.

Most people want
to have their own way
some of the time.

They do not want others
always telling them
what to do.

They do not like to be bossed.

If you are like most people,
you do not want to be bossed.

It is important to treat other people
the way you want to be treated.

If you do not like being bossed,
you should not be bossy.

Try not to be bossy.

Realize that you cannot have
your way all of the time. It
is not good for you. It is
not fair to the people around you.

Take turns deciding who will choose
what to do when you are with other people.

If you choose one activity, let the other
people choose the next activity.

Make sure you suggest an acceptable
activity when it is your turn to choose.
Choose an activity that is safe.

Be sure your parents and other
people's parents approve the activity.

Choose something that everyone will enjoy.

Be a good sport when it is the other
people's turn to choose an activity.
  Do whatever they choose to do
  if it is safe and your parents and
  the other people's parents approve.

  Try not to complain.

  Do whatever you can to make the
  activity enjoyable for everyone.

Try not to be bossy.
Do not
    bribe,
    threaten, or
    frighten
anyone into obeying you.

No one likes to be bossed.

If you do not want to be bossed,
you must not be bossy.

31

About the Author
Joy Berry is the author of more than 150 self-help books for children. She has advanced degrees and credentials in both education and human development and specializes in working with children from birth to twelve years of age. Joy is the founder of the Institute of Living Skills. She is the mother of a son, Christopher, and a daughter, Lisa.